November 2009

EARLY GERMANS

BARBARIANS!
EARLY GERMANS

KATHRYN HINDS

MARSHALL CAVENDISH · BENCHMARK · NEW YORK

To Arthur and Owen

The author and publisher specially wish to thank Peter S. Wells,
Professor of Anthropology at the University of Minnesota, Twin Cities,
for his invaluable help in reviewing the manuscript of this book.

Marshall Cavendish Benchmark 99 White Plains Road Tarrytown, New York 10591
www.marshallcavendish.us

Text copyright © 2010 by Marshall Cavendish Corporation Map copyright © 2010 by Mike Reagan

LIBRARY OF CONGRESS CATALOGING-IN-PUBLICATION DATA
Hinds, Kathryn, 1962-
Early Germans / by Kathryn Hinds.
p. cm. — (Barbarians!)
Summary: "A history of the early German peoples, who lived, traded, and fought
with the ancient Romans—covering the period from 230 BCE to 180 CE"—Provided by publisher.
Includes bibliographical references.
ISBN 978-0-7614-4064-2
1. Germanic peoples—History—Juvenile literature. 2. Rome—History—Juvenile literature.
3. Germany—History—To 843—Juvenile literature. I. Title. DD75.H56 2010 936.3—dc22 2008055789

EDITOR: Joyce Stanton PUBLISHER: Michelle Bisson ART DIRECTOR: Anahid Hamparian
SERIES DESIGNER: Michael Nelson ART RESEARCHER: Connie Gardner

Cover photo by akg-images/The Image Works

The photographs in this book are used by permission and through the courtesy of: The Image Works; akg-images: 2-3, 6, 8, 15, 16, 17, 21, 33, 35, 37, 42, 44, 50, 51, 52, 63, 64; Alinari Archives, 39, Peter Connolly/akg-images, 45, 56; Mary Evans, 46; Scheri Sueddeutsche Zeitung Photo, 55; Corbis: Elio Ciol, 27; Bettmann, 47; Werner Forman, 69; Art Resource: British Museum, 69; Bildarchive Preussicher Kulturbesitz, 1, 28; Erich Lessing, back cover, 14, 18, 26, 30, 31; Werner Forman, 13, 41, 60; Scala/Ministero per ibeni e le Attivita Cultural, 23; Art Archive; Palazzo Pitti Florence/Gianni Dagli Orti 25; The Bridgeman Art Library: Landscape on the Dachau Moor (oil on cardboard), Baum, Paul (1859-1932)/Neue Galerie, Kassel, Germany/ c Museumsland-schaft Hessen Kessel Arno Hensmanns, 16; The Conspiracy of the Batavians under Claudius Civilis, c 1666 (oil on canvas), Rembrandt Harmensz van Rijn (1606-69)/ c Nationalmuseum, Stockholm Sweden, 49; Roman/Museo Capolitino, Rome, Italy /Alinari, 66.

Printed in Malaysia
135642

cover: An 1840 illustration of the early Germanic hero Arminius leading his forces against the Romans
half-title page: A battle scene on a Roman coin minted during Rome's war against the Germanic Cimbri
    and Teutones
title page: A warrior's family greets him as he and his men return to their farmstead after a successful hunt.
back cover: A barbarian warrior defends his home from a Roman soldier. This sculptured image from Rome
    was carved in the early 100s CE.

CONTENTS

WHO WERE THE BARBARIANS?   6

1. INTRODUCING THE GERMANS   9

2. ROME UNDER THREAT   19

3. TESTING THE EMPIRE'S LIMITS   29

4. THE FIRST CENTURY   43

5. THE FRONTIER AND BEYOND   57

KEY DATES IN EARLY GERMAN HISTORY   68

GLOSSARY   70

FOR MORE INFORMATION   71

SELECTED BIBLIOGRAPHY   72

SOURCES FOR QUOTATIONS   73

INDEX   76

Who Were the Barbarians?

THE HISTORY OF THE ANCIENT WORLD IS DOMINATED BY the city-based societies of Greece, Rome, China, India, and others. Yet not far beyond the borders of these famed civilizations lived other peoples: the barbarians. They were first given this name by the ancient Greeks, imitating the sounds of languages that the Greeks found incomprehensible. Soon, though, barbarians came to be thought of not just as peoples unfamiliar with the languages and customs of Greece and

Rome, but as wild, uncivilized, uncultured peoples. This stereotype has largely endured to the present day, and the barbarian label has been applied to a variety of peoples from many parts of Europe and Asia.

The barbarians, of course, did not think of themselves this way. They had rich cultures of their own, as even some ancient writers realized. The civilized peoples both feared the barbarians

The Roman general Drusus had a vision of a woman who stopped him from completing his conquest of the Germans.

and were fascinated by them. Greek and Roman historians such as Herodotus and Tacitus investigated and described their customs, sometimes even holding them up as examples for the people of their own sophisticated societies. Moreover, the relationships between the barbarians and civilization were varied and complex. Barbarians are most famous for raiding and invading, and these were certainly among their activities. But often the barbarians were peaceable neighbors and close allies, trading with the great cities and even serving them as soldiers and contributing to their societies in other ways.

Our information about the barbarians comes from a variety of sources: archaeology, language studies, ancient and medieval historians, and later literature. Unfortunately, though, we have few records in the barbarians' own words, since most of these peoples did not leave much written material. Instead we frequently learn about them from the writings of civilizations who thought of them as strange and usually inferior, and often as enemies. But modern scholars, like detectives, have been sifting through the evidence to learn more and more about these peoples and the compelling roles they have played in the history of Europe, Asia, and even Africa. Now it's our turn to look beyond the borders of the familiar civilizations of the past and meet the barbarians.

A variety of systems of dating have been used by different cultures throughout history. Many historians now prefer to use BCE (Before Common Era) and CE (Common Era) instead of BC (Before Christ) and AD (Anno Domini), out of respect for the diversity of the world's peoples.

INTRODUCING the GERMANS

T HE EMPEROR AUGUSTUS WAS BESIDE HIMSELF AT THE NEWS. "Give me back my legions!" he roared, then wept in grief over the deaths of so many Roman soldiers. Their commander, Quinctilius Varus, had led them into an ambush. It was one of the most shameful episodes in Roman history: 15,000 highly disciplined, superbly trained soldiers slaughtered over the course of just a few days by uncivilized German tribesmen. Some twenty years earlier the poet Horace had written, "While [Augustus] lives unharmed, who would fear . . . the hordes that rough Germany breeds?" Now, in 9 CE, it appeared that the Romans didn't know "rough Germany" and its people half so well as they'd thought.

GERMANIA

Modern scholarship has shown that ancient peoples who spoke Germanic* lived in an area stretching from, in today's terms, southern

*the ancestor of modern German, Dutch, English, Danish, Swedish, Norwegian, and Icelandic

Opposite page: The German chief Arminius shocked the Roman world when he ambushed and destroyed three legions. This illustration from 1880 portrays Arminius dramatically but inaccurately—in real life he would have been wearing trousers and would not have had wings on his helmet.

9

Norway and Sweden through the Netherlands, Denmark, and Germany, and into Poland and the Czech Republic. Roman writers called this region Germania—the land of the Germans. Not all the peoples of these lands were German, however. There were other groups, too, who spoke different languages and had different cultural traditions. These peoples and the Germans often coexisted peacefully, trading and intermarrying with one another; at other times they fought over land and resources.

Germans also fought with other Germans. Although they shared many cultural traits and a common language, they did not think of themselves as a single people with shared interests. Few, if any, of these peoples would even have identified themselves as Germans. Instead they thought of themselves as members of their particular tribes, for example the Chauci, Anglii, and Gautae.

Much of Germania and many of the German peoples were unknown to the Romans, who were naturally most familiar with the lands and tribes nearest Rome's borders. Because of this, Roman writers tended to assume all Germans were basically the same. But various aspects of life differed from tribe to tribe, influenced by neighboring peoples and by the characteristics of the land itself.

The Roman historian Tacitus (56–120 CE) described Germania as "a land of fearful forest and fetid bog." This must be how it seemed to many of the Roman soldiers and merchants who traveled to the north. In reality, the territory of the early Germans was more diverse. One of its main features was the network of rivers running from south to north: the Rhine, Ems, Weser, and Elbe flowing into the North Sea, and the Oder and Vistula flowing into the Baltic Sea. The river valleys had an abundance of fertile farmland, and the rivers themselves were important routes for communication and trade.

The rivers arose in hilly, sometimes mountainous, uplands. As the rivers flowed north, the hills became gradually lower till the terrain was

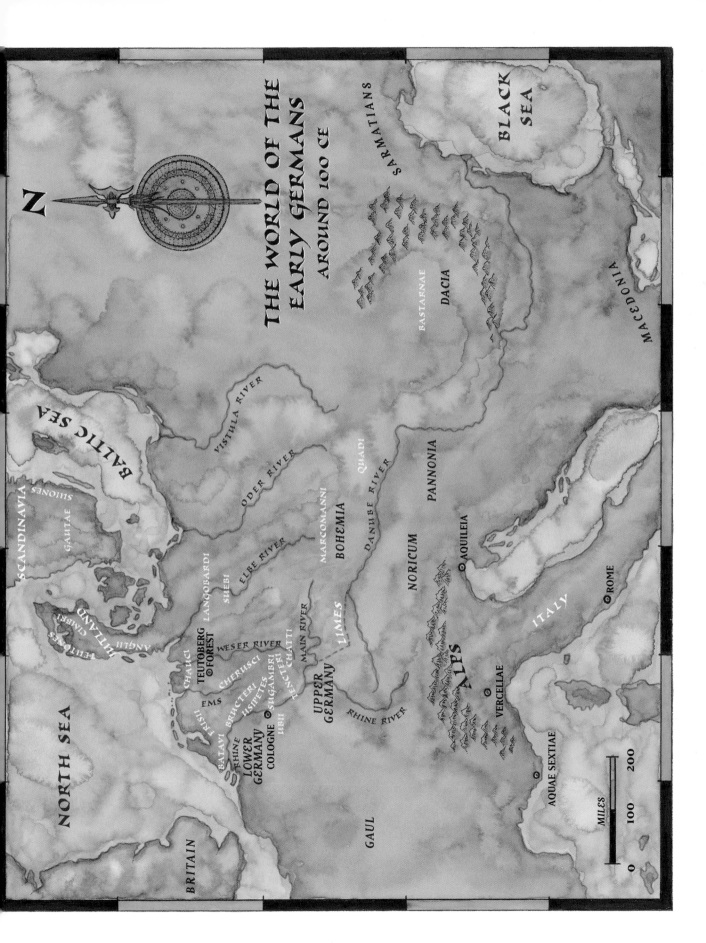

N

THE WORLD OF THE
EARLY GERMANS
AROUND 100 CE

BLACK
SEA

SARMATIANS

BASTARNAE

DACIA

MACEDONIA

VISTULA RIVER

ODER RIVER

QUADI

DANUBE RIVER

BOHEMIA

MARCOMANNI

PANNONIA

NORICUM

AQUILEIA

ELBE RIVER

SUEBI

LANGOBARDI

BALTIC SEA

SCANDINAVIA

SUIONES

GAUTAE

CIMBRI

ANGLII

TEUTONES

JUTLAND

CHAUCI

TEUTOBERG
FOREST

CHERUSCI

WESER RIVER

BRUCTERI

USIPETES

SUGAMBRI

TENCTERI

CHATTI

UBII

COLOGNE

MAIN RIVER

LIMES

UPPER
GERMANY

RHINE RIVER

NORTH SEA

BRITAIN

BATAVI

RHINE

FRISII

EMS

LOWER
GERMANY

GAUL

ITALY

ALPS

VERCELLAE

ROME

AQUAE SEXTIAE

MILES

0   100   200

A modern painting of a moor in Germany shows some of the boggy terrain that was common in ancient Germania.

mostly flat plain. West of the Elbe River, the land lay at about sea level, but was actually below sea level in some of what is now the Netherlands. This whole western region had many bogs, moors, and meadows. East of the Elbe the land remained quite flat, and often marshy, along the seacoast. Inland, however, there were many areas of low, rolling hills, often with small lakes lying in the valleys. The ground near these lakes tended to be swampy, but there was still good farmland around them.

NORTHERN WAYS OF LIFE

Over the past century, archaeology has been able to tell us much that ancient writers did not know about how German peoples lived. And archaeology has been the only way for us to learn of life in Germania before the coming of the Romans. The early Germans did not write about themselves—they passed on their history and learning orally. Only after they began to interact with Rome did they adopt writing, and for a long time they used it only for special, limited purposes. It would be centuries before the history of any of the German peoples was written down by a member of that people.

Archaeology, on the other hand, can take us back to very early times. By about 1300 BCE a splendid culture had evolved in Jutland (the peninsula that sticks up like a thumb between the North Sea and the Baltic Sea) and what is now southern Sweden. The people of this culture made magnificent objects of bronze and gold, and carved mysterious scenes of humans, animals, and ships into rock faces. These people may well have been ancestors of the Germans. Most modern scholars, however, feel it would not be accurate to refer to any of the groups living in the north as German until somewhere between 500 and 400 BCE at the earliest.

A bronze snake or sea serpent made in Jutland around 1000 BCE reveals the skill and imagination of ancient metalworkers.

IRON AGE VILLAGES

It was around this time that the northern peoples began using iron instead of bronze as their main material for tools. This was also the period that Jutland settlements took on a form that would remain common in many Germanic-speaking lands for the next thousand years or more. The earliest of these villages had about a dozen houses, all approximately the same size and with an east-west alignment. Settlements built somewhat later had as many as thirty houses, and in one case sixty. Nearly all the Jutland villages that have been studied so far were permanent settlements. Houses might be rebuilt or slightly relocated from time to time, but the community remained in basically the same place, often for centuries.

Villages like the ones in Jutland existed in other parts of Germania, too. Often they were surrounded by a wooden palisade, but additional fortifications were rare. It was also unusual for German communities to choose hilltop sites. Sometimes, however, they did take over hill forts that had been built by the Celtic peoples who earlier controlled the

This hill overlooking the upper Danube was originally fortified and occupied by Celts, but the region later became home to Germanic tribes.

eastern and southern parts of German territory. And in low-lying areas along the North Sea, villages were situated atop artificial mounds, which people built to reduce the danger of flooding.

Parts of Germania did not have the resources to support many people in a small area. In these places, settlements consisted of only a handful of families. There were also isolated farmsteads, with the nearest neighbor living some distance away. Whether standing on its own or as part of a larger community, a farmstead was typically home to a single family. The farmstead included not only the house but also outbuildings, used for storage and as workshops.

HOUSE AND FARM

A common type of dwelling was a longhouse with three aisles. Two parallel lines of wooden posts ran the length of the interior, supporting the roof and at the same time marking off the three long sections. Such a longhouse was often home to both humans and livestock: the people lived at one end and the animals at the other. Depending on the size of the house, there could be stalls for only a few animals or as many as

twenty. This was a very practical arrangement in the northern climate. Not only were the livestock sheltered from harsh weather, but their body heat helped warm the house. Otherwise the only source of heat was a rectangular open hearth in the center of the people's section.

The most important farm animals were cows, raised for their milk, meat, and leather. They could also be used to pull plows and wagons. Cattle generally accounted for 50 to 70 percent of the livestock in German settlements. Next in importance were sheep (for wool and meat), goats (for skins and meat), and pigs (for meat). Sheep and goats were favored in marshy areas, where they had no trouble grazing, while pigs were more numerous where there were woodlands, which gave them plenty of acorns and beechnuts to eat. Horses were raised in smaller numbers, but they were highly valued for riding and as status symbols.

The majority of German families supported themselves by farming: raising livestock and working the fields surrounding their village or farmstead. Barley was the most important grain crop, followed by oats. Wheat was more difficult to grow in much of Germania, but people raised it where they could. Other grains included rye and millet.

An artist's reconstruction of the inside of a German chief's three-aisled longhouse, with a fire burning in the central hearth. The swords and shields of the chief's followers hang on the wall, ready to use at a moment's notice.

A busy and prosperous farm as it may have looked around the year 200 CE

Another staple crop was flax—the seeds were nutritious and full of oil, and the stalks were processed to make linen. Farmers also grew hay to feed their cattle over the winter.

The main vegetables were peas and broad beans. There is not much evidence of gardens or orchards. People did, however, gather wild spinach, dandelion greens, lettuce, radishes, celery, blackberries, strawberries, elderberries, cherries, plums, and hazelnuts. In addition, people grew or gathered woad, a plant that made a blue dye.

Spinning, dyeing, weaving, and sewing were activities to which women devoted much time and energy. Working with wool or linen, they wove on what is called a warp-weighted loom. This was an upright loom on which the long threads (the warp) were held taut by weights tied to their ends. We know that German weavers produced some beautifully textured and patterned fabrics because we have found examples of them preserved in peat bogs. Such finds give us precious glimpses of the past, showing us aspects of German life that no Roman ever bothered to write about.

THE GENUINE SPEARMEN

THE ORIGINAL HOMELAND OF THE PEOPLE WHOM THE ROMANS DUBBED GERMANS SEEMS to have been in the area of modern Denmark, southern Sweden, and northern Germany. We have no idea what the people in this region called themselves in early times. By the time the Romans became acquainted with them, they had many different tribal names.

A nineteenth-century image of a fancifully dressed Germanic warrior armed with spear, sword, dagger, axe, and shield

So where did the name *Germans* come from? The first ancient writer to use it was Posidonius, a Greek philosopher and traveler, around 100 BCE. Some modern scholars think he may have gotten it from *gaizamannoz*, an early Germanic word meaning "spearmen." Or it could have come from a term that meant something like "fellow-countryman" or "brother." Either way, it may have been one tribe's name for itself, or perhaps for some neighboring tribe. This was pretty much what the Roman historian Tacitus, about two hundred years after Posidonius, believed. He wrote that one of the first groups to move into Gaul from east of the Rhine called themselves Germans, and then this tribal name gradually came to be applied more widely. On the other hand, the geographer Strabo, writing midway between Posidonius and Tacitus, thought the Romans came up with the term. Since the Germans were, he said, so similar to the Celtic peoples of Gaul, except for being even fiercer and taller, "The Romans . . . applied to them the name 'Germani,' as signifying 'genuine' [Celts]"—*genuine* or *true* being one possible meaning of the Latin word *germanus*.

ROME UNDER THREAT

THE FIRST GERMANS TO COME INTO CONTACT WITH THE GRECO-Roman world may have been a people called the Bastarnae, who lived along the Vistula River in the third century BCE. Greek and Roman historians weren't entirely sure about them—some thought they were Celts; others believed they were Germans. Tacitus said the Bastarnae were "like Germans in their language, mode of life, and in the permanence of their settlements." He added that they intermarried with their neighbors to the east, the nomadic Sarmatians. Modern scholars generally agree with Tacitus, but no one can be certain.

What is certain is that in 230 BCE the Bastarnae attacked a Greek colony on the Black Sea's northern shore. Thirty years later there were Bastarnae living near the lower Danube, some of them serving as mercenaries for the king of Macedonia. The Bastarnae continued to be known as mercenaries and raiders through much of the Greek world. Meanwhile, Rome was about to have its own first encounter with the Germans.

Opposite page: Roman soldiers fighting Germans and other barbarians near the lower Danube, carved in marble on the side of a Roman emperor's coffin

19

PEOPLES ON THE MOVE

Around the year 120 BCE, parts of Jutland and the neighboring North Sea coast suffered from terrible flooding, according to a number of ancient authors. If this was true, we can guess that many people saw their homes and livestock washed away, and their fields submerged by seawater. With the land's fertility destroyed by the salt, the survivors of the disaster would not have been able to support themselves. In any case, whether because of floods or other reasons, a great many people packed up and headed south in search of a place to build new lives.

Roman historians tell us the emigrants came from three main tribal groups, the Cimbri, Teutones, and Ambrones. Their migration was not easy and was destined to unsettle a large part of Europe. Wherever they went, they were regarded as invaders, and no one wanted to give them land to settle on. Since they couldn't live by farming, they took to raiding.

After a few years on the move, they reached Bohemia (part of the modern Czech Republic), home to the Celtic Boii tribe. The Boii fought them off, and they turned westward. Some Boii and other Celts may have joined them; in fact, some scholars think there was a sizable Celtic element among the three tribes almost from the beginning of their travels. In those times there was not always a clear distinction between Celtic and Germanic cultures and peoples.

Rumors about the migrating tribes began to reach Rome. In a biography of the Roman general Marius, the historian Plutarch (46–120 CE) wrote:

> At first what was reported about the numbers and strength of the invading armies seemed incredible; later it appeared that rumour fell short of the truth. Three hundred thousand armed warriors were on the march, and hordes of women and children in much greater numbers were said to be marching with them, all seeking land to support these vast hosts. . . . Their courage and daring were

irresistible; in their fighting they rushed into battle with the speed of a raging fire; nothing could stand up to them.

In 113 BCE, the emigrants attacked Noricum (today's Austria), a kingdom with strong ties to Rome. The Roman army sent to defend Noricum was quickly defeated. The Cimbri and their allies continued westward and were soon raiding the Roman province of Transalpine Gaul (now southern France). There they triumphed over each of the three Roman armies sent to repel them, first in 109 BCE, then in 107 and 105.

Next the Cimbri went into Spain, while the Teutones and Ambrones remained in Gaul. After a return to Gaul and more raiding there, the Cimbri headed north and east. Their plan was to go around the Alps, then down through the mountain pass into northeastern Italy. The Teutones and Ambrones were also set to attack Italy, which they would approach by a coastal route from the west.

An 1823 illustration shows the Roman general Marius in the thick of battle with the Cimbri at Vercellae in northern Italy.

THE FINAL BATTLES

Meanwhile, the Roman defense had been put into the hands of Marius, a famous and experienced commander. In 102 BCE he met the Teutones and Ambrones in battle at Aquae Sextiae. This was a place famous for its hot springs, where the tribesmen were relaxing and feasting. The Ambrones were the first to jump up from the meal and arm themselves. Plutarch tells us that they numbered more than 30,000 and "came forward clashing their [weapons] together rhythmically, and all leaping up together in the air, often shouting in unison their name 'Ambrones! Ambrones!'"

The Roman troops swept down on them from higher ground, forcing them back till they reached a river. A large number of Ambrones were killed beside or in the water. The rest were now in retreat. The Romans pursued them right into their camp.

Here the women came out against them, armed with swords and axes and making the most horrible shrieking, falling upon both the pursuers and the pursued—the former as their enemies, the latter as men who had betrayed them. They threw themselves into the thick of the fighting, tearing at the Romans' shields with their bare hands or clutching at their swords, and, though their bodies were gashed and wounded, they endured it to the end with unbroken spirits.

Two days later Marius did battle with the Teutones and the surviving Ambrones. His forces outmaneuvered the tribes, and the Roman victory was decisive. More than 100,000 of the Teutones and Ambrones were killed or captured. But there were still the Cimbri to deal with.
Now coming down out of the Alps, the Cimbri

were so full of confidence in themselves and of contempt for their enemies that they went out of the way to give . . . exhibitions of their strength and daring. They went naked through snowstorms, climbed to the summits of the mountains through the ice and snow drifts, and from there came tobogganing down on their broad shields, sliding over the slippery slopes and the deep crevasses.

Not far south of the Alps, they defeated the army of Marius's co-commander, Catulus, and captured a Roman fort. Then they headed deeper into Italy.

Marius and his legions rushed to aid Catulus. On a summer day in 101 BCE, the two Roman generals and their combined army faced the Cimbri on a plain near the town of Vercellae in northwest Italy. The Cimbri, said Plutarch, had the sun shining full in their faces and "were quite disheartened by the heat; they were covered in sweat and found it hard to breathe and tried to ward off the heat from their faces with their shields." The Romans, on the other hand, were not only used to hot weather but "were so tough and well trained that not a single Roman was seen to be short of breath or sweating."

Marius and Catulus won the battle, in which "the greater part of the enemy and their best warriors were cut to pieces; for in order to preserve an unbroken line those who were fighting in the front ranks were fastened together by long chains which were passed through their belts." The Cimbri women killed themselves and their children rather than be captured. According to Plutarch, the day ended with 120,000 Cimbri dead and 60,000 enslaved. The small number of emigrants left alive and free either found homes in non-Roman Gaul or returned back to the northern lands they had left so many years ago.

Having won the battle of Vercellae, Marius is carried off the field in triumph by his men. In the background Roman soldiers round up Cimbri prisoners, some of whom try to escape in their oxcarts.

CAESAR AGAINST THE BARBARIANS

The Romans had had a dread of barbarian invaders ever since Rome was sacked by a Celtic army around 390 BCE.* The migration of the Cimbri and their allies had fully reawakened those old fears. Romans kept an uneasy eye on developments to the north, feeling that a new barbarian threat could arise at any time.

In the 70s and 60s BCE there was a power struggle between two Celtic tribes, the Sequani and the Aedui, living near the border of Transalpine Gaul. The Sequani made an alliance with the Suebi, a German tribe from the other side of the Rhine River. Under the leadership of a chief named Ariovistus, fifteen thousand Suebi warriors helped the Sequani defeat the Aedui. Then Ariovistus and his men decided to settle in Gaul—in the words of Julius Caesar, they "had become enamoured of the lands and the refinement and the abundance of the Gauls, more were brought over, and there were now as many as 120,000 in Gaul."

In his *Commentaries on the Gallic War*, Caesar (who wrote of himself in the third person) explained his thoughts on the situation:

> Caesar saw it would be dangerous to the Roman people if the Germans became accustomed to crossing the Rhine, and a great body of them should occupy Gaul. He reckoned that if such wild and savage people took over the whole of Gaul, they would not feel constrained from then invading the Province [Transalpine Gaul] and thence marching into Italy itself.

In 59 BCE Caesar became governor of Transalpine Gaul, a position that put him in command of the legions stationed there. He was soon able to convince the Roman Senate of the danger posed by the Germans—and of his ability to deal with it. He then made it his business to drive Ariovistus and the other Suebi out of non-Roman Gaul.

*This event and more about the Celts are discussed in another book in this series, *Ancient Celts.*

In his biography of Caesar, Plutarch described the Germans' reaction:

> Ariovistus . . . had never imagined that Romans would attack Germans. . . . So he was now amazed at Caesar's daring, and at the same time he noticed a lack of confidence in his own men. The German spirit was still more discouraged by the prophecies made by their holy women, who used to foretell the future by observing the eddies in the rivers, and by finding signs in the whirling and in the noise of the water. These women warned them not to fight a battle until the appearance of the new moon.

A late-nineteenth-century painting of Julius Caesar wearing a triumphal crown of myrtle leaves

Caesar naturally had no intention of waiting for the new moon, and attacked the Suebi while they were still feeling discouraged. "The result," says Plutarch, "was a brilliant victory for Caesar. He pursued the enemy for forty miles, as far as the Rhine, and filled the whole of the plain with the bodies of the dead and their spoils. Ariovistus, with a few followers, succeeded in getting across the Rhine. The number of killed is said to have been 80,000."

CROSSING THE RHINE

Caesar now had a foothold in free Gaul and set about conquering it. Because the tribes were not unified against him, he was able to bring Gaul mostly under his control in less than three years. The conquest wouldn't be complete, though, till 51 BCE, thanks to uprisings and other problems. One of these problems arose in 55 BCE. Armies from two Ger-

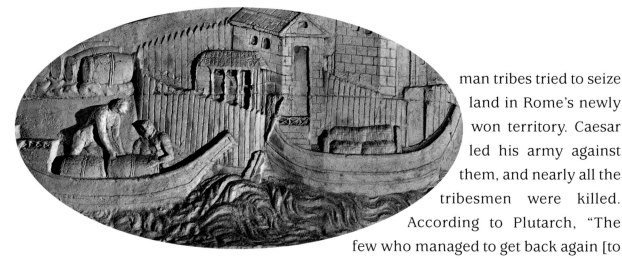

man tribes tried to seize land in Rome's newly won territory. Caesar led his army against them, and nearly all the tribesmen were killed. According to Plutarch, "The few who managed to get back again [to the other side of the Rhine] found refuge with the German tribe called the Sugambri. This gave Caesar a pretext for invading Germany, and he was in any case anxious to be the first man in history to cross the Rhine with an army." (Evidently the German armies didn't count.)

Caesar set his troops to work constructing a bridge because, in his own words, "To cross in boats would neither have befitted Caesar's own dignity nor that of Rome; even though building a bridge involved great difficulties because of the river's breadth, depth and current." The bridge was completed in ten days, and the army marched across. They spent eighteen days destroying the villages and fields of the Sugambri and their neighbors, then returned to Gaul. Once Caesar's army was back on "their" side of the river, he had the bridge destroyed.

In his *Commentaries*, Caesar made a point of portraying the Rhine as a firm boundary between Gaul and Germania. This helped support his claim that he was acting to enforce the border and so protect both Celts and Romans from the "wild and savage" Germans. In reality, the Rhine was not a line separating Celts from Germans. Instead it was a means of communication and exchange between them. Both peoples had been going back and forth across the river for generations. There were Celtic tribes living on the "German" side of the river, and Germans living on the "Celtic" side. But from Caesar's time on, the Romans would consider all peoples living east of the Rhine—regardless of their actual language and culture—to be Germans.

Rivers like the Rhine were convenient routes for trade between peoples. In this sculpture two men load a barge with barrels of wine, one of Rome's most popular exports to barbarian lands.

THE AMBER ROAD

CAESAR MAY HAVE BEEN THE FIRST ROMAN GENERAL TO CROSS THE RHINE, but Roman merchants had already done so many times. As Caesar himself said, "The Suebi give access to traders, to secure buyers for what they have captured in war." In fact, Greeks and Romans had been doing business with the Germanic world for centuries, often probably through Celtic middlemen. The north had one product that was especially sought after: amber, valued for its beauty, its scent when burned, and its reported medical and magical properties. There were many theories about amber's origin—for example that it was "a liquid produced by the rays of the sun"—but by Tacitus's time, it was known to be fossilized tree sap. He described how the people along the Baltic Sea collected amber "in the shallows, and also on the shore itself. . . . To them it is utterly useless; they gather it in its raw state, bring it to us in shapeless lumps, and marvel at the price which they receive." Traders between the Baltic and Rome followed the "Amber Road," a network of routes through the mountains north of Italy and along the Oder and Vistula rivers. Archaeologists can trace the paths of the ancient merchants thanks to finds of amber and Roman coins along the way. One discovery in particular shows us just what a big business this was: a single group of trading settlements in what is now Poland had a stockpile of more than three tons of raw amber.

This ring was carved out of amber transported down the Amber Road from the Baltic to Rome in the first century CE.

TESTING the EMPIRE'S LIMITS

I N THE DECADE AFTER THE CONQUEST OF GAUL, CAESAR WAS murdered and Rome plunged into civil war. It ended with Caesar's adopted son Augustus taking charge as sole ruler—the first emperor. Having settled affairs in Rome, he turned his attention to integrating Gaul into the empire. This meant establishing Roman-style cities, building roads, setting up a tax system—and making sure all of that was safe from German raiding. As Caesar had written, for the Germans "no shame is associated with banditry, providing it happens outside a tribe's own territory. Indeed they look on it as training for war, which keeps the young men active and alert. When a chieftain decides to lead a raid, those who volunteer to go with him are cheered by all."

UNEASY NEIGHBORS

For some years Augustus was content with maintaining the Rhine as the border between the Roman and barbarian worlds, while still allowing communication between them. At least one tribe, the Ubii, became

Opposite page: Arminius portrayed as a seventeenth-century knight by a German artist of that time. The Cherusci leader was adopted as a national hero by Germans of many eras.

so enthusiastic about the Roman way of life that it asked permission to settle in Gaul as an ally of Rome. Since the Ubii would help protect the frontier from other Germans, their request was granted. Their settlement on the west bank of the Rhine eventually grew into the city of Cologne (from Latin *colonia*, meaning a town founded by the state for defensive purposes).

Trade also carried on across the Rhine—there was plenty of demand for Roman goods in Germania. But in 17 BCE members of the Sugambri, Usipetes, and Tencteri tribes killed some Roman merchants for trespassing on their territory. After this they began a series of raids on Gaul. In the course of their uprising, they ambushed a Roman patrol. The encounter developed into a full-scale battle against a legion commanded by Marcus Lollius. Not only were the Romans defeated, but the Germans captured their standard—a golden eagle, every legion's symbol of Roman pride.

A legion's gold eagle standard was a rallying point and symbol of pride for Roman soldiers, but a tempting target for Rome's enemies in battle.

This humiliating incident was Rome's excuse to undertake the conquest of Germania. Already some forts were under construction along the Rhine; more were begun, and further plans were made. In 12 BCE Augustus's stepson Drusus began the campaign. Some of his forces sailed down the Rhine and out into the North Sea—where no Roman had ever gone before—to explore all the river mouths to the east. He was looking for as many ways into Germania as possible.

The next year Drusus crossed the Rhine and advanced to the Weser, along the way invading Sugambri territory. The ancient historian Cassius

Dio explained, "He was able to do this because the Sugambri, angry with the Chatti, the only tribe among their neighbours that had refused to join their alliance, had campaigned against them with all their population. Seizing this opportunity, he passed through their land unnoticed."

With each year's campaigning, Drusus and his troops advanced deeper into Germania. In 9 BCE they reached the banks of the Elbe River, where Drusus died after a fall from his horse. Command passed to his brother, Tiberius, who led the legions in battle after battle between the Rhine and the Weser for the next two years. Tiberius went into retirement from 6 BCE to 4 CE, but during his absence other generals kept up the task of subduing the German tribes.

Little is known about these years, but it seems Augustus believed at least part of Germania was pacified enough to become a province. There were plenty of forts, and the beginnings of civilian towns. (The ruins of one such town, complete with markets and a civic center, were discovered by archaeologists in 1997 about sixty miles east of the Rhine.) The behavior of some of the German tribes also suggests that the Romans were really settling in—it was becoming increasingly common for German communities to join together in large tribal groupings, the better to stand up to Rome's advances.

Drusus, who received the triumphal title Germanicus because of his victories against the Germans

The Marcomanni, for example, were a tribe that originally lived along the Main River near where it flowed into the Rhine. Their chief Maroboduus had been to Rome as a child or young man, educated alongside the emperor's own grandsons.* He returned to his people

*Augustus often made it a practice to have leaders of conquered or allied peoples send their sons to Rome to be educated under his supervision. The boys learned Roman values while also serving as hostages for their people's good behavior.

with firsthand knowledge of Roman ways. So when Roman troops marched through Marcomanni territory, Maroboduus knew what was coming. Velleius Paterculus, who served as a soldier under Tiberius, later wrote about Maroboduus:

> A man of noble family, strong in body and courageous in mind, a barbarian by birth but not in intelligence, he achieved among his countrymen no mere chief's position gained as the result of internal disorders or chance . . . but, conceiving in his mind the idea of a definite empire and royal powers, he resolved to remove his [tribe] far away from the Romans and to migrate to a place where . . . he might make his [people] all-powerful.

Maroboduus settled in Bohemia and began building a coalition of tribes. By 6 CE he was powerful enough to worry Augustus—in Rome it was rumored that he had a standing army of more than 70,000 men. Tiberius was on the verge of leading a campaign against him, when a revolt erupted in two of the empire's eastern European provinces. Tiberius, needing to put down the rebellion, signed a hasty peace treaty with Maroboduus. As part of the treaty, Maroboduus probably promised not to interfere in Roman affairs—even if there was an uprising in Germania.

"THE DISTURBER OF GERMANY"

This was how Tacitus referred to the German leader Arminius.* Before the events that earned him that nickname, Arminius was actually a member of the Roman army. This was not a rare thing. During the conquest of Gaul, Caesar had begun the practice of recruiting German warriors to serve as mercenaries and auxiliary troops, and other generals

*This is the romanized form of his German name, which may have been something like Erminameraz. Earlier scholars believed *Arminius* was a Latin version of *Hermann*, but language experts today think this is unlikely.

had continued it. Young warriors soon found they could earn glory and good money fighting for Rome.

The Romans also commonly required a people who signed a peace treaty with them to supply the army with troops. This is probably how Arminius came to serve. His tribe, the Cherusci, was subdued by Tiberius in 4 CE and then apparently agreed to become allies of Rome. In any case, Arminius ended up commanding a group of Cheruscan auxiliaries in Tiberius's army. As a result he was granted Roman citizenship and what we might call a knighthood.

Arminius's service in the Roman military taught him how the legions worked—and how they might be defeated.

It seems likely that the soldier-historian Velleius Paterculus met Arminius while they were both fighting in Tiberius's campaign to put down the rebellions in eastern Europe. Velleius later described Arminius as "a young man of noble birth, brave in action and alert in mind, possessing an intelligence quite beyond the ordinary barbarian; he . . . showed in his countenance and in his eyes the fire of the mind within." Arminius even became fluent in Latin, the Roman language. He appeared to be just the sort of barbarian Rome could use.

One way that the empire increased its power was by recognizing some leaders of conquered or allied peoples as "friends of Rome." This special status was reinforced with money, gifts of luxury goods, and flattery. The theory was that eventually these friendly leaders would feel they had more in common with the Romans than with their own people. And it would be in the leaders' personal interests to keep the peace and to encourage the adoption of Roman ways in their territory. When Arminius returned to Germania in 7 or 8 CE, he seemed ready to do exactly as Rome expected.

SEEDS OF DISCONTENT

The situation Arminius came home to was described by Cassius Dio: "The Romans had by now established themselves in parts of Germany, wintering there and founding cities. On their side the barbarians had begun to accept Roman ways: holding markets and peaceful meetings. But they had not forgotten their ancestral customs. Nor had they lost their sense of freedom." Arminius also found a new Roman governor in place, Quinctilius Varus, who "tried to force the pace of change, dishing out orders as if to slaves and squeezing money as if from docile subjects."

Even worse was Varus's attitude toward the people he governed. According to Velleius, "he entertained the notion that the Germans were a people who were men only in limbs and voice"—subhuman, in other words. Not surprisingly, many German leaders were longing for their former power, while many of the common people decided they preferred their old way of life to one dominated by foreigners.

Varus made it his special concern to promote Roman law in the province. The Germans played along "by trumping up a series of fictitious lawsuits, now provoking one another to disputes, and now expressing their gratitude that Roman justice was settling these disputes." So, as described by Velleius, the Germans flattered Varus into a false sense of security even as they planned to rebel.

Arminius and his father, Segimer, were soon at the heart of the plot. They spent plenty of time with Varus, often dining with him, convincing him of their friendship and their loyalty to Rome. Meanwhile Arminius was organizing the German forces for attack. With his knowledge of Varus and his experience of Roman military practices, he was able to craft the perfect trap.

ARMINIUS'S VICTORY

In 9 CE, at the end of summer, everything was ready. Varus had spent the season handing down judgments in Cherusci territory, near the

Weser River. Now as he headed back toward the Rhine for the winter, he received news of an uprising to the north. The site was far from any Roman forts. Nevertheless, Varus detoured his whole column, including not only three legions but also the women, children, and servants who traveled with them, along with a large number of pack animals and wagons.

Varus thought the territory he was passing through was friendly to him. Moreover, he had Arminius and Segimer as escorts. But Arminius and Segimer soon left, saying they were off to scout ahead. They went immediately to where their troops were waiting and led them against the nearest Roman detachments, killing them all.

Mounted on a white horse, Arminius fights his way toward Varus (in red on the far right) in the Battle of the Teutoberg Forest, as imagined by a nineteenth-century artist.

Next they came down on Varus and the main body of soldiers, who were working their way through rough, wooded terrain. It was already hard going, and then a storm with violent wind and pouring rain made it worse. The Germans attacked from all sides. Dio tells the story:

> At first it was hit-and-run, with spears hurled from a distance; but when they could see that many were being wounded and there was no serious counter-attack, they began to press closer. By now the column was in chaos, with soldiers, wagons and civilians all jumbled up: impossible to organize into defensive formations. . . . On the second day things went better. Despite losses, they broke through to open country. But on the third morning the column plunged once more into forest and began to take the heaviest casualties yet. There was no room to deploy the cavalry among the trees, or use infantry and cavalry in unison.

The fourth day brought more fierce wind and rain. The Romans found it "difficult even to stand. Wet bowstrings, slippery spears and sodden shields deprived them of effective use of their weapons; while the Germans, more lightly armed, fared better." As the Romans weakened, still more Germans joined the attack.

With his defeat certain, Varus killed himself. German warriors later found his body, and Arminius sent the head to Maroboduus in Bohemia, as if to show him it was possible to defeat Rome. Maroboduus declined to join in Arminius's war, and had the head taken to Augustus for decent burial. But the emperor no doubt understood Arminius's message.

The four-day conflict has become known as the Battle of the Teutoberg Forest. The Romans called it the Varian Disaster, blaming Varus for leading so many Romans into harm's way. Three legions were

Arminius's men gather in a sacred grove to present him with trophies from their victory over Varus's legions.

utterly wiped out, leaving Augustus in the mournful state we met him in on p. 9.

Augustus had more than just the legions' destruction to lament. After the Teutoberg Forest, Arminius and his forces destroyed nearly all Roman forts and settlements east of the Rhine. The Romans had lost the province of Germania.

ROMAN REVENGE

Because of the Varian Disaster, Augustus gave up hope of extending his empire. He died in 14 CE, leaving behind a will in which he advised his successor, Tiberius, "that the empire should be confined to its present limits," bounded by the Rhine and Danube rivers. Nevertheless, a new German campaign was under way. Its leader was Tiberius's nephew Germanicus, whose father, Drusus, had commanded Rome's forces in Germania in 12–9 BCE.

Germanicus, fired with enthusiasm, probably believed he could recover the province. But even if he couldn't, Rome would have the satisfaction of striking back at the barbarians. In his first two years of campaigning, he went after the tribes that had been allied with Arminius, practically annihilating one of them. But the people he most wanted to punish were the Cherusci, Arminius's own tribe.

Germanicus was probably aware that there were now serious divisions among the Cherusci. The two main factions were led by Arminius and Segestes—"famous, respectively, for treachery and loyalty towards us," in the words of Tacitus. Segestes had even tried to warn Varus about Arminius's plot. Although he had not been listened to, he remained staunchly pro-Roman. According to Tacitus, he explained his position this way: "I held that Romans and Germans have the same interests, and that peace is better than war." In addition, Segestes hated Arminius for eloping with his daughter, Thusnelda, whom he had promised to someone else.

In 15 CE Germanicus got a message from Segestes, begging for help because he was under attack by Arminius's faction. Germanicus rescued Segestes and in the course of the battle captured Thusnelda, who "exhibited the spirit of her husband rather than of her father." Segestes admitted that he had been holding her in his camp by force, but "from her there came no appeals, no submissive tears; she stood still, her hands clasped inside her robe, staring down at her pregnant body."

Arminius, wrote Tacitus, "was driven to frenzy by the seizure of his wife and the foredooming to slavery of his wife's unborn child. . . . 'Noble the father,' he would say, 'mighty the general, brave the army which, with such strength, has carried off one weak woman. . . . Not by treachery, not against pregnant women, but openly against armed men do I wage war.'" Indeed, outrage at the capture of Thusnelda seems to have united the Cherusci behind Arminius, and neighboring tribes also rallied to his cause.

The Germans ambushed some of Germanicus's forces, but after three days of hard fighting, the Romans managed to get away to safety. The next year the Romans again faced Arminius and his allies. Although Arminius was wounded during the battle, he escaped alive. Numerous other German warriors were killed, however, and Germanicus claimed victory. Then Tiberius, deciding enough had been accomplished in Germania, recalled his nephew to Rome. The next year he awarded Germanicus a triumphal procession, in which Thusnelda and her son were paraded as captives. They lived the rest of their lives in Italy, never seeing Arminius again.

This statue of a sorrowful German woman was probably sculpted between 110 and 120 CE. In 1841 it was identified as a portrayal of Thusnelda.

LAST STANDS

Arminius was soon engaged in another war, this time with Maroboduus. Both men were now leaders of powerful tribal confederations. Tacitus wrote, "The strength of these two nations, the valour of their chiefs were equal. But the title of king rendered Maroboduus hated among his countrymen, while Arminius was regarded with favour, as the champion of freedom." As a result, some members of Maroboduus's kingdom, including the Langobardi tribe, went over to Arminius. Tacitus explained, "The Cherusci and Langobardi were fighting for ancient renown or newly-won freedom; the other side for the increase of their dominion." But after the first battle, Maroboduus retreated, and many of his allies deserted him. Eventually he fled to Italy.

Now without a rival, Arminius seems to have tried to enlarge his confederation, even to create a kingdom of his own. There may have been several reasons for this, including a craving for power and a desire to unify the tribes of Germania to withstand any future Roman invasions. But traditionally, German peoples had had a single, absolute ruler only in times of war. During peacetime they generally preferred to be governed by tribal councils. Arminius's ambition was too much for "his countrymen's independent spirit," and he was killed "by the treachery of his kinsmen."

Tacitus, writing his *Annals* in the early second century, concluded the story of Arminius with this tribute: "He was unmistakably the liberator of Germany. Challenger of Rome—not in its infancy, like kings and commanders before him, but at the height of its power—he had fought undecided battles, and never lost a war. He had ruled for twelve of his thirty-seven years. To this day the tribes sing of him."

DURING THE COURSE OF HIS CAMPAIGN IN 15 CE, GERMANICUS MADE A PILGRIMAGE to the site of the Varian Disaster. Guided to the place by some of the few who'd escaped, he gave the remains of the dead proper burial and funeral rites. He also heard the survivors' stories of some of the horrific things they'd seen, including Roman prisoners being sacrificed to the Germans' god of war.

SACRIFICES AND BOG BODIES

Human sacrifice was part of German religion as it was among most ancient peoples (including the Romans). In Germania the commonest type of sacrifice, though, probably was throwing offerings into pools of water or bogs. This can be seen by the large number of objects found in bogs in what are now Denmark and northern Germany, including jewelry, a great many Roman weapons, and even boats and carts. Human sacrifice was likely reserved only for especially solemn holidays or during times of great need, such as warfare or famine.

Sacrificed people, like the offerings of weapons and jewelry, often ended up in bogs. Usually they had been killed first, and at least some of them may have offered themselves willingly. One well-preserved "bog body," known as Tollund Man, is famous for the look of deep peace on his face. Before his death, he had eaten a meal consisting of a variety of grains and seeds. Scientists have found a number of other bog bodies with the same stomach contents, so this last meal was probably part of a religious ceremony before the sacrifice.

Tollund Man was found in a Danish bog in 1950. Probably a member of the noble class, he died around 200 CE, strangled before his body was laid in the bog.

Of the hundreds of bog bodies so far discovered, it is hard to tell how many were sacrifices (willing or otherwise), since drowning in bogs was also used as a punishment for certain crimes. But from the German point of view, these deaths, too, may have been sacrifices for the good of the tribe.

The FIRST CENTURY

W HEN TIBERIUS RECALLED GERMANICUS IN 16 CE, HE WAS MORE
or less admitting it was impossible to hold the lands from the
Rhine to the Elbe. With previous conquests, the empire usually had
taken over other empires or kingdoms—places that already had cities,
money, organized taxation, roads of some sort, and other features of
civilization. In general the common people of the conquered lands sim-
ply exchanged one ruler for another and saw little difference in their
daily lives.

Most Germans, however, had a very different attitude toward kings,
as we have seen. Germans also tended to dislike living in cities; it was
said they referred to them as "tombs surrounded by nets." Before contact with Rome, they had no experience with money. For Rome to rule
Germania, it had to start from scratch—and given the limits of tech-
nology and communications in the ancient world, this was just too
large a task, even for the mighty empire. But that didn't mean Rome
was completely done with Germania.

Opposite page:
A third-century
Frank and a
first-century
Sugambrian.
The nineteenth-
century artist
portrayed these
German warriors
as primitive sav-
ages—especially
the Sugambrian,
with his wicker
shield and rough
fur garment.
This was a bar-
barian stereo-
type that went all
the way back to
ancient Rome.

43

Romans, Germans, soldiers, and civilians mingle in a marketplace near a Roman frontier fort.

NORTH SEA REBELLIONS

Since 13 BCE a wide swath of land from eastern Gaul to the Rhine had been a military zone where several legions were stationed. The northern part of this frontier area was known as Lower Germany; the southern part was called Upper Germany. Part of Lower Germany lay along the North Sea coast east of the Rhine.

There were not only soldiers but also many civilians living in the military zone. Some came from Italy or the provinces. Others were natives of Gaul or Germania. German tribes living on the west bank of the Rhine were integrated into the empire. Roman forces patrolled parts of the east bank of the river, and seem to have reserved some areas for raising crops and livestock. Germans living close to the Rhine, on either side, therefore had frequent contact with Romans.

Most interactions were peaceful—and profitable. Tacitus wrote of "traders from our provinces who had been attracted to an enemy's land . . .

first by the freedom of commerce, next by the desire of amassing wealth." Nevertheless, as Tacitus indicated, the free tribes of Germania were still generally looked on as "the enemy." Even among tribes that had treaties with Rome, there was no guarantee of permanent peace.

An artist's reconstruction of barracks and stables excavated on the site of a Roman fort near the Danube in southern Germany.

TOO MANY TAXES

The Frisii were a tribe living along the North Sea just east of the Rhine. They had been subdued by Drusus during his campaign of 12 BCE, and he made a treaty with them recognizing them as allies of Rome. In return, they were required to pay an annual tribute, or tax, of a certain number of ox hides. These hides were used by the military to make tents and other items.*

The Frisii paid their tribute without any problem for more than two decades. "No one ever severely scrutinized the size or thickness" of the hides, wrote Tacitus. But then a new military governor arrived. Decid-

*Scholars have estimated that it took about 54,000 calfskins to make tents for a single legion.

ing to set some standards, he demanded hides as large and thick as those of wild bulls. Perhaps he was hoping the Frisii could get some of the animals Caesar had described:

> These are a little below the elephant in size, and of the appearance, colour, and shape of a bull. Their strength and speed are extraordinary. . . . These the Germans take with much pains in pits and kill them. The young men harden themselves with this exercise, and practice themselves in this kind of hunting, and those who have slain the greatest number of them . . . receive great praise.

Caesar was talking about aurochs, a kind of wild cattle that are now extinct—but they were nowhere near the size of elephants. Yet they were much larger than modern cows, which in turn are much larger than those raised in ancient Germania. So, as Tacitus commented, the

Ancient Germans hunting an aurochs. The illustrator has accurately portrayed the animal's size, strength, and fierceness. None of the hunters, however, would have worn a horned helmet—in fact, helmets were rarely worn at all by the early Germans.

new tribute "would have been hard for any nation, and it was the less tolerable to the Germans, whose . . . home cattle are undersized."

When the Frisii couldn't pay their tribute, the governor seized herds and lands. Then, apparently, he took Frisian women and children to sell as slaves. The Frisii protested, but received no relief. In 28 CE they rebelled, seizing and hanging the soldiers who came to collect the tribute. The governor fled to a fortress near the sea, and the Frisii besieged it. In the battle that followed, the Frisii killed more than 1,300 Roman soldiers.

Tacitus sums up the result: "The Frisian name thus became famous in Germany, and Tiberius kept our losses a secret. . . . Nor did the Senate care whether dishonour fell on the extreme frontiers of the empire." Rome no longer tried to hold on to the bit of Lower Germany east of the Rhine.

RESTLESS TRIBES

There was trouble with the Frisii again in 58 CE. Tacitus told how they "moved up their youth to the forests and swamps, and their non-fighting population . . . to the river-bank, and established themselves in unoccupied lands, reserved for the use of our soldiers, under the leadership of Verritus and Malorix, the kings of the tribe, as far as Germans are under kings." The Roman governor threatened an attack unless the Frisii left this area, but Verritus and Malorix would not give in. The governor therefore sent them to Rome to make their case before the emperor Nero himself. After a round of sightseeing and a visit to the theater, the two Germans met with Nero. He granted them Roman citizenship, then without warning sent in an auxiliary cavalry unit to drive the Frisii off the territory they'd claimed.

This seems to have been a time of turmoil in much of Germania, with many cases of tribes going to war against one another. An especially tragic story, told by Tacitus, was that of the Ampsivarii. Having been driven off their lands by another tribe, they tried to claim the territory the Romans had evicted the Frisii from. One of the Ampsivarii leaders, Boiocalus, met with the governor of Lower Germany and made an eloquent plea that his people be given the land.

The governor's public response was "that people must submit to the rule of their betters; that the gods . . . had willed [that] the decision as to what should be given or taken from them was to rest with the Romans." Privately, the governor told Boiocalus that because of the help he had given Rome during the war with Arminius, he could have the territory he wanted. But Boiocalus "spurned the offer as the price of treason, adding, 'We may lack a land to live in, we cannot lack one to die in.'" The Ampsivarii never found a home, and "after long wanderings, as destitute outcasts, . . . their entire youth were slain in a strange land, and all who could not fight, were apportioned as booty"—in other words, enslaved.

OFFENDED AUXILIARIES

The Batavians, a tribe in what is now the Netherlands, had been allies of Rome since the time of Augustus. They paid no tribute but instead supplied the empire with crack auxiliary troops, some of whom even served as the emperor's bodyguard. But in 68 CE the emperor Nero committed suicide. He was succeeded by a general named Galba, who dismissed the Batavian guards. This action offended the entire tribe. The Batavians became angrier still when Vitellius, commander of the legions in Lower Germany, ordered all young Batavian men to join the army.

A Batavian noble and former auxiliary officer named Civilis decided the time had come to rise against Rome. He invited "the chiefs of the nation and the boldest spirits of the lower class" to a sacred grove for a feast, and they all swore to join his cause. Neighboring tribes, including the Frisii, soon became part of the rebellion as well. Batavians and

This is how Rembrandt, the great seventeenth-century Dutch artist, envisioned Civilis and the other Batavian leaders swearing to support each other in their rebellion against Rome.

many other Germans serving in Rome's army and navy deserted and went over to Civilis.

The Batavian Revolt lasted more than a year. Tacitus described the struggle in his *History*, giving vivid impressions of much that happened during this turbulent time. On one occasion, Civilis dammed part of the Rhine to flood a field near his camp because "the Roman soldier is heavily armed and afraid to swim, while the German, who is accustomed to rivers, is favoured by the lightness of his equipment and [his] height." Sure enough, when the Romans attacked Civilis's camp, "a panic arose, when they saw arms and horses swallowed up in the vast depths of the marshes. The Germans leapt lightly through the well-known shallows."

Civilis's uprising eventually involved most of the German tribes living near the Rhine. A number of Roman forts were burned, and the legions were thrown into confusion. The Germans owed their successes largely to Civilis's knowledge of Roman tactics, but also to the fact that Rome itself was in chaos. During the year 69 Galba was assassinated, his successor committed suicide, and then Vitellius and a general named Vespasian were each proclaimed emperor by the legions they commanded.

Vespasian won out, and officially became emperor on December 20, 69. The next spring he sent forces against Civilis. After a series of battles, the Roman commander offered to negotiate—perhaps because during part of the rebellion, Civilis had claimed to be fighting against Vitellius on behalf of Vespasian. According to Tacitus, most of the Batavi were now tired of this war: "'We can no longer,' they said, 'postpone our ruin. . . . What has been accomplished by destroying legions with fire and sword, but that more legions and stronger have been brought up?'" It seems likely that Civilis accepted the offer of peace for his people, and a pardon for himself. But we may never know exactly what happened to him, because the rest of Tacitus's *History* has been lost.

THE LITTLE GOLDEN BOOK

A 1764 portrait of Tacitus, who is widely regarded as the greatest of Roman historians

Another book by Tacitus, missing for centuries, was rediscovered in 1451. Called *Germania*, scholars considered it such a precious find that they nicknamed it *libellus aureus*—"the little golden book." No other known work by any ancient author made such a complete study of European peoples outside the worlds of Greece and Rome. Tacitus, who wrote *Germania* around 98 CE, had probably never been to the north himself. But he had access to firsthand accounts by people who had traveled, traded, or fought there. Nearly all these sources are now lost, so we are lucky to have Tacitus's information.

We need to bear in mind, however, that he wrote for a sophisticated Roman audience. This means he put things in terms his readers would understand, and of course he shared many of their biases. He sometimes stereotyped the Germans; for example: "All have fierce blue eyes, red hair, huge frames, fit only for a sudden exertion. They are less able to bear laborious work." But Tacitus also thought most of his fellow Romans were *too* sophisticated. He sometimes portrayed the Germans as "noble savages" as a way of pointing out what he saw as corruption and self-indulgence in his own people.

Germania described many aspects of Germanic society. Tacitus was naturally interested in military matters, pointing out that the Germans rarely wielded swords but instead carried spears that could be used for either throwing or thrusting. Few warriors had armor or helmets; for defense they depended mainly on their shields, which were colorfully painted. When Germans went into battle they had a special war song or yell—"not so much an articulate sound, as a general cry of valor. They aim chiefly at a harsh note and a confused roar, putting their shields to their mouths, so that, by reverberation, it may swell into a fuller and deeper sound."

Squadrons and battalions were formed of men who were all related to each other, which Tacitus believed inspired them with extra courage. Moreover, their wives and children remained close by during battle: "They are to every man the most sacred witnesses of his bravery—they are his most generous applauders. The soldier brings his wounds to mother and wife, who shrink not from counting . . . them and who administer food and encouragement." If the warriors seemed to be giving way before the enemy, the women reminded them of their duty and urged them to fight harder.

The women of the tribe help their men prepare for battle in an illustration from a German history book published in 1823.

Although men were the heads of families, women were highly respected. They often managed not only the household but the farm as well. Moreover, it was felt that women had a special holiness and spirit of prophecy, so their advice and opinions were taken very seriously.

To depict this early German family as accurately as possible, the artist worked from archaeological finds and ancient Roman images of Germanic peoples.

Some women were singled out for particular reverence. For instance, in both *Germania* and his *History*, Tacitus wrote about Veleda, a woman of the Bructeri tribe who lived in a high tower. Widely regarded as almost a goddess, she was able to settle disputes between different tribes and prophesied many of Civilis's successes during the Batavian Revolt.

Unlike upper-class Roman women, German women nursed their own babies. The children, Tacitus said, grew up "with those stout frames and limbs which we so much admire." When a boy came of age, his father, another male relative, or a chief presented him with a shield and spear in a public ceremony. After receiving their arms, young men often joined the retinue of a chief. Tacitus explained:

> It is no shame to be seen among a chief's followers. . . . These followers vie keenly with each other as to who shall rank first with his chief, the chiefs as to who shall have the most numerous and the bravest followers. . . . When they go into battle, it is a disgrace for the chief to be surpassed in valour, a disgrace for his followers not to equal the valour of the chief. . . . To defend, to protect him, to ascribe one's own brave deeds to his renown, is the height of loyalty. The chief fights for victory; his vassals fight for their chief.

Chiefs paid their followers for their services by giving them banquets, horses, and weapons—all funded by the loot they took in wars and raids. When they were not fighting, they spent most of their time (according to Tacitus) sleeping, hunting, feasting, gambling, and enjoying entertainments. For example, "One . . . kind of spectacle is always exhibited at every gathering. [Young men] who practise the sport bound in the dance amid swords and lances that threaten their lives. Experience gives them skill and skill again gives grace; profit or pay are out of the question; however reckless their pastime, its reward is the pleasure of the spectators."

Peacetime had its duties as well as pleasures. Every new or full moon, a council of chiefs met to discuss any matters of concern to the community. Major decisions, however, had to be approved by the entire tribe. When everyone was assembled, the priests called for quiet. The chiefs then spoke in turn, according to age, rank, or reputation. If the people didn't like what they heard, they just grumbled among themselves. When they approved of something, however, they did so loudly, the men brandishing their spears. Tacitus explained that a chief was listened to "more because he has influence to persuade than because he has power to command." Even in war, "the generals do more by example than by authority. If they are energetic, if they are conspicuous, if they fight in the front, they lead because they are admired."

Germania is a short book, but full of so many interesting subjects, it is difficult to summarize. Along with the topics we have already looked at, Tacitus described the importance of hospitality, the common occurrence of feuds, the punishments for crimes. He noted that the Germans made beer, that they sometimes decorated their houses with colored clay, that they took warm baths almost every day. He wrote about women's linen dresses with purple embroidery and the way Suebian men wore their hair twisted into a knot on top of or at the side of the head. He even had information about the Suiones of Scandinavia, who were "powerful in ships" (their descendants would be the Vikings), and about a neighboring tribe that was ruled by a woman. But beyond the Suiones lay an almost motionless sea, and "only thus far . . . does the world extend."

WE HAVE ALREADY ENCOUNTERED SEVERAL ASPECTS OF ANCIENT GERMAN RELIGION, such as sacrifices and the prophecies of holy women. But who were the gods of Germania? Tacitus wrote that the Germans believed their deities were too grand to enclose in buildings or to portray in human form, so they worshipped them in forests and groves, "giving divine names to mysterious and invisible spirits." Among these spirits, he said, were deities like the Egyptian goddess Isis and the Roman gods Mercury, Hercules, and Mars—gods of

EARLY GERMAN RELIGION

intelligence, strength, and war respectively. Modern scholars believe Tacitus was referring to Wodan, Donar, and Tiwaz, known in the later mythology of the Vikings as Odin, Thor, and Tyr. The goddess mentioned by Tacitus may have been Nehalennia, a deity of abundance who, like Isis, was also associated with ships and the sea.

In a very famous section of *Germania*, Tacitus described another powerful goddess, Nerthus, who he thought was Mother Earth. Honored by tribes of the southwestern Baltic Sea region, she was said to live in a sacred grove on an island. A wagon was kept there, covered with a cloth. At certain times of year the priest of Nerthus sensed the goddess's presence in the wagon, had it hitched up to a pair of cows, and led it out among the people. "Then follow days of rejoicing and merrymaking in every place she condescends to visit. . . . No one goes to war, no one takes up arms; every iron object is locked away. Then, and then only, are peace and quiet known and welcomed, until the goddess . . . is restored to her sacred [place] by the priest."

Barbarian peoples living close to the frontier often adopted some Roman customs, including religious ones, such as making statues of deities. This was a portrayal of the mother goddess of a tribe living near the Rhine.

The FRONTIER and BEYOND

BY THE END OF THE FIRST CENTURY, UPPER AND LOWER GERMANY had been upgraded from military zones to full provinces. Moreover, the emperor Domitian had closed a corridor between the Rhine and the Danube through which German peoples had been able to cross into Roman territory. A 340-mile boundary called the *limes* now stretched from the middle Rhine to the upper Danube. Initially this was just a string of watchtowers along a strip of cleared ground. Then forts were built, and in the 120s a nine-foot-high wooden palisade was added. Earthworks completed the fortifications in the 150s. The *limes* helped the empire protect its border and keep an eye on its northern neighbors. But although it was a visible frontier between the Roman and barbarian worlds, it did not completely separate them.

PEACEFUL COEXISTENCE
Rome actively pursued treaties with tribes beyond the border so that they wouldn't raid the empire and would also discourage other tribes

Opposite page: It took more than 100,000 Roman troops to man the Rhine-Danube frontier. This watchtower is being built within view of others, seen atop the bluffs in the background. Each had stacks of hay next to it, which would be set afire to signal its neighbors that there was trouble in the area.

57

from doing so. Many tactics were used to guarantee friendly relations, including cash payments and valuable gifts to tribal leaders. Sometimes Rome also gave tribes special trading privileges and promises of protection against enemies. Occasionally they even granted them lands within the empire.

When a tribe's friendship was doubtful, the Romans might provide a leader of their own choosing. In the mid-first century, for example, the emperor Claudius sent Arminius's nephew Italicus, "with a present of money," to rule the Cherusci. Italicus's father had been an auxiliary commander who remained loyal to Rome and even fought against Arminius during Germanicus's campaigns. This episode also shows how the empire used the principle of "divide and conquer," keeping tribes and even families from uniting against it.

SOLDIERS AND LOCALS

Hiring soldiers from the tribes was another way to create and cement loyalty to Rome. During the first and second centuries, the number of German auxiliaries in the Roman army seems to have continually increased. Auxiliaries served for at least twenty years, at the end of which they received Roman citizenship. Many German men returned home after completing their service. They brought back wealth and a storehouse of experience, which typically earned them great respect in their communities. Archaeologists have found numerous ex-auxiliaries buried with their Roman swords and armor, along with rich grave goods showing the men's high status.

Auxiliaries were among the troops who manned border forts. Sometimes auxiliaries were recruited from nearby tribes. In many cases, however, auxiliary units were sent to distant provinces. This might be because those particular men's skills were needed in a certain place or because they were less likely to cause trouble far from home. In any case, soldiers on the frontier, whether they were legionaries or auxil-

iaries, generally spent far more time on patrol and similar duties than in actual fighting. They had many opportunities for peaceful interactions with the local people.

Over the course of time, villages and towns grew up near the forts. The residents included merchants and craftspeople from Italy and the provinces as well as from free Germania. There were around 110,000 soldiers stationed along the frontier, and they needed all kinds of supplies, from food and raw materials to pottery and tools to cloth and leather. The army had its own craftsmen to produce much of its military equipment, but most of the other needs had to be met by the communities around the forts. Roman soldiers therefore did a great deal of business with the area's residents, and probably became friends with some of them. It was also common for soldiers and local women to form long-term relationships. All these types of personal contact promoted sharing between Roman and Germanic cultures.

A third-century sculpture shows residents of a town in one of the German provinces making their payments to a Roman tax collector.

ONE OF THE MOST INTERESTING PRODUCTS OF CONTACT BETWEEN ROMANS AND Germans may have been the futhark. This was a Germanic alphabet that seems to have taken shape in the first or second century CE. Its letters are known as runes, and the first six—ᚠ ᚢ ᚦ ᚨ ᚱ ᚲ— stand for the sounds *f*, *u*, *th*, *a*, *r*, and *k*, giving the alphabet its name. Many scholars believe an individual or group of people set about creating this symbol system after meeting Romans and seeing how they used writing. We can imagine the runes' inventors being determined to have letters that their own people could use, to express their own language in their own way.

RUNES

The futhark seems to have originated in the western Baltic, where the earliest and most numerous runic inscriptions have been found. In the first centuries of their use, runes were most commonly engraved on weapons and on women's jewelry, often marking the object with the name of its maker or owner. Sometimes a runic inscription was a magical or religious formula, dedicating the object to a particular purpose or deity. It is possible that runes were also used in divination, to discover the will of the gods. Tacitus tells us that sometimes when divine guidance was needed, "A little bough is lopped off a fruit-bearing tree, and cut into small pieces; these are distinguished by certain marks, and thrown . . . over a white garment." Then a priest or, in family matters, the father randomly chose three of the wooden pieces and interpreted the marks on them. We cannot say for certain the symbols were runes, but it seems likely—or perhaps these symbols helped inspire the runes' creation. In any case, the futhark went on to have a long history as a system for both communication and divination.

Above: This is said to be the oldest runic inscription in Sweden,
carved into stone probably during the second century CE.

TRADE AND CHANGE

Archaeologists have discovered thousands of Roman goods through-out Germania, some brought home by auxiliaries and most of the rest products of trade. In the region nearest the frontier, where there were regular, direct dealings between Romans and Germans, many every-day Roman objects have been found. So have large numbers of Roman coins, bearing out Tacitus's comment that "the Germans nearest us value gold and silver for their use in trade, and recognize and prefer certain types of Roman coins." Farther away, the Roman products that reached Germania were mainly luxury goods, such as silver and gold jewelry, and bronze, silver, and glass feasting and wine-drinking equip-ment. Other Roman imports to Germania included perishable items such as grain and wine.

Among the goods German merchants offered in exchange were amber, furs, down, and women's hair (blond wigs were extremely fash-ionable in Rome). The biggest business, however, was in slaves. In the Roman Empire, more than 250,000 slaves were bought every year. Slaves did a large proportion of the empire's manual labor, keeping farms and factories running, turning mill wheels, mining metals, wait-ing on the wealthy, fighting in gladiator shows, and more. When the empire was waging wars, especially wars of conquest, there were plenty of captured enemies who could be enslaved. But the demand for slaves did not slack off in times of peace. German tribes soon found it very profitable to sell their prisoners of war to Roman slave traders—so prof-itable that some tribes began raiding others solely to get captives.

Slavery was practiced in Germania, but not on a large scale, and slaves were treated very differently than in Rome. Tacitus, struck by the contrast, wrote that among the Germans, the average slave "has the management of a house and home of his own. The master requires from the slave a certain quantity of grain, of cattle, and of clothing, as he would from a tenant, and this is the limit of subjection." Slave raids and Roman-style slavery were clearly a massive shock to the communities and individuals affected.

Catering to the needs of the frontier army bases also spurred far-reaching changes. An example can be seen in a settlement along the North Sea about 150 miles from the Rhine. During the late first century BCE it had only five farmsteads, all the same size, with a total of ninety-eight stalls for livestock. Over the next hundred years the settlement grew, and so did the number of Roman imports found there. Moreover, some people began living in bigger houses.

By the end of the first century CE one farmstead was much larger than the others and was even surrounded by its own palisade. The house had a bigger main hall and a special area where objects were crafted from bronze and iron. Numerous Roman goods were found on this property, including coins, jewelry, glassware, high-quality pottery, and even a fan with an ivory handle. At the settlement's peak, there were enough stalls for 443 animals. Scholars theorize that the villagers must have been raising cattle to provide the Roman soldiers with meat and leather, and that one family played a dominant role in running this enterprise and so became particularly wealthy and important. Similar developments occurred in numerous other German communities.

This was a huge change from when Caesar first encountered the Germans. He had been amazed to find they seemed to have little interest in wealth, or even in land ownership:

Nor has any one a fixed quantity of land [to farm] or his own individual limits; but the . . . leading men each apportion to the tribes and families . . . as much land as . . . they think proper, and the year after compel them to move elsewhere. For this enactment they advance many reasons . . . lest they be anxious to acquire extensive estates, and the more powerful drive the

weaker from their possessions . . . [and] lest the desire of wealth spring up, from which cause divisions and discords arise; and that they may keep the common people in a contented state of mind, when each sees his own means placed on an equality with those of the most powerful.

An artist of the 1930s imagined that the capital of the Chatti tribe, near the upper Weser River, may have looked much like this in the early first century CE.

Roman influence overcame the old ways of life in much of Germania. This fed unrest in many tribes—often because people wanted access to more Roman goods, wanted to share in Roman material wealth, wanted to live more like Romans. And some wanted all of that, plus Roman lands.

NEW UPHEAVALS

In 162 members of the Chatti and Chauci tribes tried to move into Upper Germany. They were driven back, but Rome's military strength was weakening. Many of the legions were away fighting in Persia. Soldiers returning from this war brought with them a deadly plague, which

MARRIAGE IN GERMANIA

IN ANCIENT ROME, MARRIAGE WAS A VERY UNEQUAL PARTNERSHIP, ESPECIALLY AMONG the upper classes. Husbands were the legal guardians of their wives, who were regarded more or less as children by the law. In fact, most brides were only teenagers, while their husbands (chosen by their fathers) were typically at least ten years older. But in Germania, according to Tacitus, "The young men marry late. . . . Nor are the maidens hurried into marriage; the same age and a similar stature is required; well-matched and vigorous they wed." The whole subject of German marriage was a fascinating one to Tacitus, beginning with the wedding:

An 1823 illustration of Tacitus's description of a wedding in Germania. In reality, though, the men would almost certainly have been dressed in their best tunics and trousers.

The parents and relatives are present, and pass judgment on the marriage-gifts, gifts not meant to suit a woman's taste, nor such as a bride would deck herself with, but oxen, a caparisoned steed, a shield, a lance, and a sword. With these presents the wife is espoused, and she herself in her turn brings her husband a gift of arms. This they count their strongest bond of union, these their sacred mysteries, these their gods of marriage. Lest the woman should think herself to stand apart from aspirations after noble deeds and from the perils of war, she is reminded by the ceremony which inaugurates marriage that she is her husband's partner in toil and danger, destined to suffer and to dare with him alike both in peace and in war. The yoked oxen, the harnessed steed, the gift of arms proclaim this fact. She must live and die with the feeling that she is receiving what she must hand down to her children neither tarnished nor depreciated, what future daughters-in-law may receive, and may be so passed on to her grandchildren.

had devastating effects on the empire. The frontier was extremely vulnerable, and many tribes took advantage of this fact.

Some 6,000 Langobardi and Ubii crossed the Danube in 166. They were overcome, agreed to peace terms, and returned to their own lands. Around the same time another group of Germans almost reached Italy before they, too, were defeated. This force differed from previous German warrior bands, according to Cassius Dio: "Among the corpses of the barbarians there were found even women's bodies in armour."

This was the beginning of nearly fifteen years of intense warfare between Rome and the tribes beyond the Danube. The conflict has become known as the Marcomannic Wars, since the Marcomanni, along with the Quadi, were the main peoples involved. In all, however, there were about twenty-five tribes fighting the empire. The threat was so serious that the emperor Marcus Aurelius went in person to the Danube region to command the troops. His first task, however, was to deal with a Sarmatian tribe that was threatening the Roman province of Dacia (modern Romania).*

While Marcus Aurelius was in Dacia, the king of the Marcomanni, Ballomar, led his coalition of tribes into the province of Pannonia (now Hungary). In 170 they inflicted a severe defeat on the Roman defenders, killing or wounding 20,000 legionaries and auxiliaries. After plundering Pannonia, they forged ahead into Italy itself—the first barbarians to do so since the Cimbri and Teutones. Ballomar besieged the city of Aquileia, which was finally rescued by Roman forces in 171.

The Marcomanni were driven back, but it was obvious that the Danube was no longer a secure border. For the rest of the decade, with only brief lulls of peace, Marcus Aurelius fought the Germans and Sarmatians along and even beyond the Danube. By the time he died in 180, he had succeeded in containing the barbarian threat. Military force naturally played a strong role, but so did diplomacy. Marcus Aurelius nego-

*For more on the Sarmatians, see *Scythians and Sarmatians*, another book in this series.

Conquered Germans kneel before the emperor Marcus Aurelius, stretching out their hands to beg for Rome's mercy. In Roman eyes, this was the proper relationship between the empire and its barbarian neighbors— but it was not a relationship that would last.

tiated a variety of treaties. Some tribes were required to supply auxiliary troops; some were made allies; some were even given Roman lands to settle on. The empire had bought itself a little more time.

In the aftermath of the Marcomannic Wars, however, things continued to change in Germania. Over the next century or so, the trend grew for tribes to join together in confederations. These large groupings included the Franks along the Rhine, the Saxons by the North Sea, the Alemanni near the upper Danube, and to the east the Burgundians and the Goths. Like the Marcomanni and their allies, these coalitions would come to want Roman lands and the Roman way of life. Many would pursue their goals through warfare, leading the fourth-century Roman historian Ammianus Marcellinus to refer to "the Germans, our ferocious and implacable foe." But peaceful interactions between Romans and barbarians continued, too. A new culture was developing, one that gradually blended Roman and Germanic elements—both part of the western European heritage that influences us even today.

KEY DATES IN EARLY GERMAN HISTORY

230 BCE Bastarnae attack a Greek colony on the Black Sea's northern shore

120 BCE approximate date of the beginning of the migration of the Cimbri, Teutones, and Ambrones

113 BCE Cimbri, Teutones, and Ambrones attack Noricum and defeat a Roman army

109, 107, 105 BCE Cimbri, Teutones, and Ambrones defeat Roman armies in Gaul

102 BCE Marius defeats Teutones and Ambrones at Battle of Aquae Sextiae

101 BCE Marius defeats Cimbri at Battle of Vercellae

60s BCE Ariovistus leads Suebi warriors into Gaul

59 BCE Caesar defeats Ariovistus and begins conquest of Gaul

55 BCE Caesar crosses the Rhine and campaigns against German tribes for 18 days

17 BCE Sugambri, Usipetes, and Tencteri warriors conduct raids in Gaul and defeat a Roman legion (the Lollian Disaster)

12 BCE Drusus begins campaigning in Germania

9 BCE Drusus dies and Tiberius takes over the campaign against the Germans

4 CE Tiberius subdues Arminius's tribe, the Cherusci

6 CE Tiberius signs a treaty with Maroboduus, ruler of the Marcomanni tribe

9 CE Arminius destroys three Roman legions (the Varian Disaster)

14 CE Tiberius becomes emperor; Germanicus begins his campaign against the Germans

A second-century clay mask portrays a German man with his hair twisted into a knot in the Suebian style.

15 CE	Arminius's wife is taken prisoner by the Romans; Arminius ambushes and nearly defeats Roman forces
16 CE	Arminius is wounded in battle against the Romans, and Germanicus claims victory; Tiberius recalls Germanicus to Rome
17 CE	Arminius's wife and son are paraded in Germanicus's triumphal procession; Arminius and Maroboduus go to war against each other
18 CE	Maroboduus flees to Italy
19 CE	Arminius is betrayed and killed by some of his relatives
28 CE	Frisii tribe rebels against Roman rule
58 CE	Frisian leaders visit Rome; Roman governor rejects Ampsivarii tribe's request for land along the Rhine
68—70 CE	Batavian Revolt, led by Civilis
98 CE	approximate date of Tacitus's *Germania*; the *limes* is established around this time
150s CE	completion of the last stage of fortifying the *limes*
162 CE	Chatti and Chauci tribes trying to move into Upper Germany are driven back by Rome
166 CE	beginning of Marcomannic Wars between Rome and tribes beyond the Danube
170 CE	Ballomar, king of the Marcomanni, leads a coalition of tribes into Roman territory
171 CE	Ballomar's forces driven out of northern Italy
180 CE	end of Marcomannic Wars

Augustus advertised his power with this coin showing a grateful barbarian holding out a baby for the imperial blessing.

GLOSSARY

auxiliaries In the Roman army, forces made up of non-Romans from the provinces or from peoples with whom Rome had treaties.

cavalry Soldiers who fought on horseback.

Celtic Refers to a family of languages that includes modern Welsh and Irish, to speakers of Celtic languages, to the lands where Celtic languages were or are spoken, or to the cultures of those peoples and lands. In the third century BCE Celtic speakers occupied a large portion of Europe, from Ireland to what is now Turkey.

farmstead A complex including a house and buildings for storage and other purposes, often surrounded by a low fence or wall, where a single family lived and processed crops they raised in nearby fields.

Gaul The Roman name for the Celtic territory between the Pyrenees Mountains, the Alps, and the Rhine River—modern France, Belgium, and Luxembourg; most of Switzerland; and the westernmost parts of Germany and of the Netherlands. Southern Gaul came under Roman rule in 118 BCE; Julius Caesar conquered the rest in the 50s BCE.

legion A unit of the Roman army. In Augustus's time each legion probably had about 5,500 men.

mercenaries Soldiers who hire out their services to anyone willing to pay.

Sarmatians A nomadic people from the region north of the Black Sea.

staple A crop that is heavily relied on, usually as a mainstay of the diet.

FOR MORE INFORMATION

BOOKS

Deem, James M. *Bodies from the Bog.* Boston: Houghton Mifflin, 2003.

Markel, Rita J. *The Fall of the Roman Empire.* Minneapolis: Twenty-First Century Books, 2007.

Wilcox, Peter, and Rafael Treviño. *Barbarians Against Rome: Rome's Celtic, Germanic, Spanish, and Gallic Enemies.* Oxford: Osprey Publishing, 2000.

WEB SITES

Livius Articles on Ancient History. *Germania Inferior.*
http://www.livius.org/germinf.html

The National Museum of Denmark. *Danish Prehistory.*
http://www.nationalmuseet.dk/sw33830.asp

Nydam Bog.
http://www.nydam.nu/eng/nydambog.html

Silkeborg Public Library et al. *The Tollund Man: A Face from Prehistoric Denmark.*
http://www.tollundman.dk/

UNRV History. *Tacitus: Germania.*
http://www.unrv.com/tacitus/tacitusgermania.php

SELECTED BIBLIOGRAPHY

Cassius Dio. *Roman History.* Translated by Earnest Cary. Online at http://penelope.uchicago.edu/Thayer/E/Roman/Texts/Cassius_Dio/home.html

Cunliffe, Barry, ed. *Prehistoric Europe: An Illustrated History.* New York: Oxford University Press, 1994.

Davidson, H. R. Ellis. *Gods and Myths of Northern Europe.* New York: Penguin Books, 1964.

Froncek, Thomas. *The Northmen.* New York: Time-Life Books, 1974.

Jones, Terry, and Alan Ereira. *Terry Jones' Barbarians.* London: BBC Books, 2006.

McCullough, David Willis, ed. *Chronicles of the Barbarians: Firsthand Accounts of Pillage and Conquest, From the Ancient World to the Fall of Constantinople.* New York: Times Books, 1998.

Murdoch, Adrian. *Rome's Greatest Defeat: Massacre in the Teutoburg Forest.* Stroud, Gloucestershire: Sutton, 2006.

Pliny the Elder. *The Natural History.* Translated by John Bostock. Online at http://www.perseus.tufts.edu/cgi-bin/ptext?lookup=Plin.+Nat.+toc

Plutarch. *Fall of the Roman Republic.* Translated by Rex Warner. New York: Penguin Books, 1958.

Tacitus. *The Annals.* Translated by Alfred John Church and William Jackson Brodribb. Online at http://www.perseus.tufts.edu/cgi-bin/ptext?lookup=Tac.+Ann.+toc

——. *Germania.* Translated by Alfred John Church and William Jackson Brodribb. Online at http://www.perseus.tufts.edu/cgi-bin/ptext?lookup=Tac.+Ger.+toc

——. *The History.* Translated by Alfred John Church and William Jackson Brodribb. Online at http://www.perseus.tufts.edu/cgi-bin/ptext?lookup=Tac.+Hist.+toc

Todd, Malcolm. *The Early Germans.* 2nd ed. Malden, MA: Blackwell Publishing, 2004.

———. *The Northern Barbarians 100 BC–AD 300.* rev. ed. New York: Basil Blackwell, 1987.

Velleius Paterculus. *The Roman History.* Translated by Frederick W. Shipley. Online at http://penelope.uchicago.edu/Thayer/E/Roman/Texts/Velleius_Paterculus/home.html

Wells, Peter S. *The Barbarians Speak: How the Conquered Peoples Shaped Roman Europe.* Princeton, NJ: Princeton University Press, 1999.

Williams, Derek. *Romans and Barbarians: Four Views from the Empire's Edge.* New York: St. Martin's Press, 1998.

SOURCES FOR QUOTATIONS

Chapter 1

p. 9 "Give me back": Murdoch, *Rome's Greatest Defeat*, p. 125.

p. 9 "While [Augustus] lives": ibid., p. 25.

p. 10 "a land of fearful": Williams, *Romans and Barbarians*, p. 74.

p. 17 "The Romans . . . applied": McCullough, *Chronicles of the Barbarians*, p. 11.

Chapter 2

p. 19 "like Germans": McCullough, *Chronicles of the Barbarians*, p. 98.

p. 20 "At first what was": Plutarch, *Fall of the Roman Republic*, pp. 23–24.

p. 21 "came forward clashing": ibid., p. 32.

p. 22 "Here the women": ibid., pp. 32-33.

p. 22 "were so full": ibid., pp. 35–36.

p. 23 "were quite disheartened" and "were so tough": ibid., p. 39.

p. 23 "the greater part": ibid., p. 40.

p. 24 "had become enamoured": Jones, *Barbarians*, p. 85.

p. 24 "Caesar saw it would be": ibid., p. 86.

p. 25 "Ariovistus . . . had never" and "The result": Plutarch, *Fall of the Roman Republic*, p. 263.

p. 26 "The few who managed": ibid., p. 266.

p. 26 "To cross in boats": Williams, *Romans and Barbarians*, p. 69.

p. 27 "The Suebi give": Todd, *The Northern Barbarians*, p. 22.

p. 27 "a liquid produced": Pliny, *Natural History* 37.11.

p. 27 "in the shallows": McCullough, *Chronicles of the Barbarians*, p. 97.

Chapter 3

p. 29 "no shame": Williams, *Romans and Barbarians*, pp. 80–81.

p. 31 "He was able": Murdoch, *Rome's Greatest Defeat*, p. 34.

p. 32 "A man of noble": Velleius Paterculus, *The Roman History* 2.108.

p. 32 "the disturber of Germany": Tacitus, *Annals* 1.55.

p. 33 "a young man": Velleius Paterculus, *The Roman History* 2.118.

p. 34 "The Romans had" and "tried to force": Williams, *Romans and Barbarians*, p. 95.

p. 34 "he entertained": Velleius Paterculus, *The Roman History* 2.117.

p. 34 "by trumping up": ibid. 2.118.

p. 36 "At first it was" and "difficult even": Williams, *Romans and Barbarians*, p. 98.

p. 38 "that the empire": Tacitus, *Annals* 1.11.

p. 38 "famous, respectively": ibid. 1.55.

p. 38 "I held that": ibid. 1.58.

p. 39 "exhibited the spirit": ibid. 1.57.

p. 39 "from her there came": Jones, *Barbarians*, p. 94.

p. 39 "was driven to frenzy": Tacitus, *Annals* 1.59.

p. 40 "The strength": Tacitus, *Annals* 2.44.

p. 40 "The Cherusci and Langobardi": ibid. 2.46.

p. 40 "his countrymen's" and "by the treachery": ibid. 2.88.

p. 40 "He was unmistakably": Jones, *Barbarians*, p. 98.

Chapter 4

p. 43 "tombs surrounded": Murdoch, *Rome's Greatest Defeat*, p. 121.

p. 44 "traders from our provinces": Tacitus, *Annals* 2.62.

p. 45 "No one ever": ibid. 4.72.

p. 46 "These are a little": McCullough, *Chronicles of the Barbarians*, p. 76.

p. 47 "would have been hard": Tacitus, *Annals* 4.72.

p. 47 "The Frisian name": ibid. 4.74.

p. 47 "moved up their youth": ibid. 13.54.

p. 48 "that people must," "spurned the offer," and "after long wanderings": ibid. 13.56.

p. 48 "the chiefs of the nation": Tacitus, *The History* 4.14.

p. 49 "the Roman soldier": ibid. 5.14.

p. 49 "a panic arose": ibid. 5.15.

p. 50 "'We can no longer'": ibid. 5.25.

p. 50 "All have fierce": Tacitus, *Germania* 4.

p. 51 "not so much": ibid. 3.

p. 51 "They are to every man": ibid. 7.

p. 53 "with those stout": ibid. 20.

p. 53 "It is no shame": ibid. 13–14.

p. 53 "One . . . kind of spectacle": ibid. 24.

p. 54 "more because he has": ibid. 11.

p. 54 "the generals do more": ibid. 7.

p. 54 "powerful in ships": ibid. 44.

p. 54 "only thus far": ibid. 45.

p. 55 "giving divine names": Williams, *Romans and Barbarians*, p. 82.

p. 55 "Then follow days": Froncek, *The Northmen*, p. 144.

Chapter 5

p. 58 "with a present": Murdoch, *Rome's Greatest Defeat*, p. 93.

p. 60 "A little bough": Tacitus, *Germania* 10.

p. 61 "the Germans nearest": Cunliffe, *Prehistoric Europe*, p. 442.

p. 61 "has the management": Tacitus, *Germania* 25.

p. 62 "Nor has any one": McCullough, *Chronicles of the Barbarians*, pp. 73–74.

p. 64 "The young men marry": Tacitus, *Germania* 20.

p. 64 "The parents and relatives": ibid. 18.

p. 65 "Among the corpses": Cassius Dio, *Roman History* 72.3.2.

p. 67 "the Germans, our ferocious": Williams, *Romans and Barbarians*, p. 115.

INDEX

Page numbers for illustrations are in boldface

Map, 11

alphabet, Germanic, 60, **60**
amber, 27, **27**
Ammianus Marcellinus (historian), 67
animals
  farm, 14–15
  hunting, 46–47, **46**
  stables, **45**
Ariovistus (tribal chief), 24–25
Arminius (German chief), **8**, **28**, 32–36, **33**, **35**, **37**, 38–40
army, Roman, 58–59
Augustus (emperor), 9, 29, 30, 31, 36, 38, 48

Ballomar (tribal king), 65
Batavian Revolt, 48–50, **49**
bogs, 41, **41**
Boiocalus (German leader), 48

Caesar, Julius, 24–26, **25**, 27, 29
Cassius Dio (historian), 30–31, 34, 36, 65
Catulus (general), 22–23
Celtic tribes, 19, 20, 26
children, German, 53
Civilis (Batavian leader), 48–50, **49**
Claudius (emperor), 58
Commentaries on the Gallic War (Caesar), 24, 26

divide and conquer, principle of, 58

Domitian (emperor), 57
Drusus (brother of Tiberius),
    30–31, **31**, 38, 45

family, German, 51, **52**, 53
farms, 14–16, **15**, **16**, 62
first century, **42**, 43
    Batavians, 48–50, **49**
    North Sea rebellions, 44–45
    restless tribes, 47–48
    taxes, 45–47
    forts, Roman, 57, 59
    frontier and beyond, **56**, 57
    frontier army bases, 62
    new upheavals, 63, 65, **66**, 67
    peaceful coexistence, 57–58
    soldiers and locals, 58–59, **59**
    trade and change, 61–63

Galba (emperor), 48, 49
Gaul, 30
Germania (Tacitus), **50**, 50–51,
    53–54, 55
Germanicus, 38–39, 41, 43
Germans, early
    Batavian Revolt, 48–50, **49**
    Germania and, **8**, 9–10, **11**, 12,
    12
    Germanic society, 50–51, **51**,
    52, 53–54
    iron age villages, 13–14, **13**

key dates in history, 68–69
in Marcomannic Wars, 65, 67
North Sea coast inhabitants,
    44–45, **44**, **45**
and Northern way of life,
    12–13
Roman conquest of Germania,
    29–32, **31**, 38–40, **39**
gods and goddesses, German, 55,
    55

homes, Germanic
    and farms, 14–16, **15**, **16**
    villages, 13–14, **14**, 59
Horace (poet), 9

iron, 13–14, **13**

limes (boundary), 57
longhouses, 14–15, **15**

Marcomannic Wars, 65, 67
Marcus Aurelius (emperor), 65,
    66, 67
Marius (general), 20–23, **21**, **23**
Maroboduus (tribal chief), 31–32,
    36, 40

Nero (emperor), 47, 48
North Sea rebellions, 44–45

plague, 63, 65

Plutarch (historian), 20–23, 25, 26

Posidonius (philosopher), 17

religion, early German, 55, **55**

Rome, 9, **18**, 19

  Arminius and victory over, 32–36, **33**, **35**, **37**, 38

  battles for Roman defense, 21–23, **23**

  Caesar against the barbarians, 24–25, **25**

  Caesar crossing the Rhine, 25–26, **26**

  conquest of Germania, 29–32, **31**

  legion's gold eagle standard, 30, **31**

  Marcomannic Wars, 65, 67

  migrating tribes, 20–21, **21**

  Roman army, 58–59

  in tribal warfare, 63, 65, **66**, 67

runic inscriptions, 60, **60**

sacrifices, human, 41

Segestes (German warrior), 38–39

slavery, 61–62

Strabo (geographer), 17

Tacitus (historian), **50**

  on Arminius, 32, 38, 39, 40

  description of Germania, 10

  on early German religion, 55, 60

  on first German-Roman contact, 19

  Germania, 50–51, 53–54, 55

  History, 49, 50

  on North Sea coast inhabitants, 44–45

  on origin of "German" name, 17

  on taxes, 46–47

  on trade, 61

Teutoberg Forest, Battle of the, 34–36, **35**, **37**, 38

Thusnelda (wife of Arminius), 38–39, **39**

Tiberius (emperor), 31, 32, 33, 38, 39, 43, 46–47

Tollund Man (bog body), 41, **41**

trade

  across the Rhine River, 30

  Amber Road, 27, **27**

  and change, 61–63

tributes (taxes), 45–47

  tax collector, **59**

Varian Disaster, 36, 38, 41

Varus, Quinctilius (Roman commander), 9, 34–36, **35**, 38

Velleius Paterculus (soldier-
    historian), 32, 33, 34
Vespasian (emperor), 49–50
villages, iron age, 13–14, **14**
Vitellius (commander), 48, 49, 50

warriors, German, 17, **17**, **42**
  Arminius, **8**, **28**, 32–36, **33**, **35**,
    37, 38–40
watchtowers, **56**, 57
women, German, 22, 23, 51, **51**,
    52, 53

ABOUT THE AUTHOR

Kathryn Hinds grew up near Rochester, NY. She studied music and writing at Barnard College, and went on to do graduate work in comparative literature and medieval studies at the City University of New York. She has written more than forty books for young people, including *Everyday Life in Medieval Europe* and the books in the series LIFE IN THE MEDIEVAL MUSLIM WORLD, LIFE IN ELIZABETHAN ENGLAND, LIFE IN ANCIENT EGYPT, LIFE IN THE ROMAN EMPIRE, and LIFE IN THE RENAISSANCE. Kathryn lives in the north Georgia mountains with her husband, their son, and an assortment of cats and dogs. When she is not reading or writing, she enjoys dancing, gardening, knitting, playing music, and taking walks in the woods. Visit Kathryn online at www.kathrynhinds.com